HOW TO HEAR THE PREACHING OF GOD'S WORD WITH PROFIT

by Stephen Egerton

with chapters by C. Matthew McMahon

I0170012

Copyright Information

How to Hear the Preaching of God's Word with Profit by Stephen Egerton with chapters by C. Matthew McMahon
Edited by Therese B. McMahon

Published by Puritan Publications
A Ministry of A Puritan's Mind® in Crossville, TN.
www.apuritansmind.com
www.puritanpublications.com

This Print Edition, 2019
Electronic Edition, 2019

Manufactured in the United States of America

ISBN: 978-1-62663-329-2
eISBN: 978-1-62663-328-5

Table of Contents

Do You Hear the Lord's Voice?
by C. Matthew McMahon, Ph.D.

Micah 6:9. "The LORD'S voice cries to the city-wisdom shall see your name: "Hear the rod! Who has appointed it?"

Congregations today do not think of the act of preaching in the way God requires them to think about it. They seem to forget, or disassociate, the preacher *with* God, and there is a great attempt at making the preaching of the word simply good advice. However, the biblical mandate is that God's prophet, herald, messenger, angel or pastor is in fact, God's *mouth*. When the preacher preaches God's word, *God is talking* to the people.

In the book of Micah, the prophet by the same name is uncompromising and bold in his delivery of God's message throughout every chapter. Ministers of God *ought* to be bold, plain and faithful in their communication of divine truth. Why? They *are* the mouth of God.

The city the prophet cries to is Jerusalem, the center of worship – the church. The crying, or *cries*, is preaching the truth, or preaching doctrine. God does not *whisper* in preaching to his people, he *cries* out to them. When the text says, "Wisdom shall see your name," it means that wise is the man who hears the solemn and grave words of the preacher and acts on them in walking justly and loving mercy. In this case, the wise man who hears the words of the preacher in all gravity, discerns God's judgment in the "rod". Micah preaches chastisement to a wayward people; *it is God's voice*. It has ties to salvation. It is still *God's voice*. Those who are wise to hear the voice of the preacher, discern God's intent in the message of God's deliverance for the people.

The voice of the Lord by the herald cries to the city to stir them up to repentance. Whoever is wise will see the name of the Lord *in* that herald and acknowledge him to be his messenger no matter what "the word" of the Lord is in the mouth of the preacher. In this case, the message was the rod of judgment for their sin. But it could, in fact, be any message God desires to proclaim to his people according to his word.

Consider, then, that God's people should hear the crying voice of the Lord in the preaching of all true ministers. In the case of God against his people in Micah 6, "hear the rod," was the message. It was a corrective and disciplinary judgment against the wayward acts of the church's failure to worship from a right heart. But this may not always be the case. Ministers preach and teach God's word to the people on varied occasions with many different messages. Yet, no matter what the occasion is, if the minister is faithfully heralding the word of God, God's people should hear those sermons as if it is *the voice of the Lord himself.* Do Christians really do that? Do they really perceive it in that way? Do you?

The voice of the Lord is in all faithful sermons given by all faithful ministers. The Lord's voice *can* be found there. The Lord's voice *cries* in such preaching. There is a famous passage of Scripture that compliments this one in Micah. "For this reason we also thank God without ceasing, because when you received the word of God which you heard from us, you welcomed it not as the word of men, but as it is in truth, the word of God, which also effectively works in you who believe," (1 Thess. 2:13). The preached word is given by prophets, heralds, messengers, interpreters, elders, pastors, or preachers. These are those who are called and qualified and set apart. There is great importance to discern the call, those appointed and those qualified in this official role. Is this not of grave importance for the church? The harvest is plentiful, but the workers few. But if your church is going to install a minister, just make *sure they are true workers!* Such preaching and teaching from these heralds about the word of God are to be regarded by Christians as *God speaking.* When God's word is preached, Christians are to discern God's voice in its cries. Where does this happen? It happens *in* the voice of the preacher.

True ministers point people to Christ, the Living Word, the Living Voice of God, in the power of God's Spirit for the edification of the people of God. And if one is a beloved sheep of Christ's fold, this is said of them, "My sheep hear My voice, and I know them, and they follow Me," (John 10:27). The voice of Christ in this way is a glorious voice, mighty in its operation, dividing the very soul and spirit, of a man, (Heb. 4:12).

What is it, then, to *hear* the Lord's voice? The Hebrew of the text in Micah is both hear it *and* obey it, a combination. One does not really hear if they are not willing to do what the voice of the Lord says. Obedience is tied to real hearing. It is not enough for the passage of Scripture, God's voice, to be threaded through the ear canal. It must be externally heard and spiritually understood. It must move the Christian to action. It must correct wayward behavior and bring the Christian back to the path of salvation. "Hear the Rod!" For all intents and purposes, this is what church discipline is about.

You might hear many things in a sermon, but to what *end* do you hear? What good comes from your hearing? Does God's voice simply please you in some way for a time, some kind of religious feeling that's needful for appeasing your conscience? Do you simply feel as though you have done your duty? Do you increase in knowledge and understanding, but you never grow one *iota* in stature to be conformed into the image of Christ? Have you heard the words on the page but never heard the voice of the Lord in your heart? We do not look to ministers simply to occupy our time for a moment, just to externally move us to another emotional moment. Preaching the word ought to be seen by you as getting closer to heaven or closer to hell every Sunday. You may sit under a minister of the word, and he may preach many wonderful points of divinity to you, and many moral truths against drunkenness, swearing, profaning the Sabbath, deceit, cheating, worldliness, *etc.* You may sit a very long time under such a minister, and God may be patient with you, though you may not obey the voice of the minister. Like the parable of the wedding feast, Luke 14:16-17, many were invited, but they had other things on their mind; farms, oxen, family business. God says, *they do not hear the voice of my minister, I will never let them, then, taste of my feast.* Remember, *Judas* heard all of Christ's sermons.

Rev. Stephen Egerton, in this most excellent treatise, will show you what your duty is in considering hearing the word of God preached. In the first chapter he considers what it means to have your ear *bored* by God as you commit to "taking heed" to hearing the word as you ought. As Christ said, "Take heed therefore how ye hear," (Luke 8:18). Then, he gives general duties in chapter 2 in relationship to any preparations that ought to be made before coming to hear the sermon. Chapter 3 deals with what the hearer ought to do while hearing the sermon. And chapter 4 deals with the duties of the Christian after the sermon, lest, as he says, "Is not the hearer discharged of his duty when he has heard the whole sermon attentively? No, although there is scarcely one of a hundred who does not think so."

Egerton reminds me, in the way he lays out this work, and its simplicity, of Michael Harrison.[1] Both of these men took great pains in their preaching to be comprehensive, and then after their preaching, they summarized their works into short, manageable treatises for their churches. Why did they do this? In their respective congregations, they wanted their people to be reminded of the most important aspects of the truth in their doctrines and sermons as a whole. It is equally sad that both of these men have no other works available. The sermons which made up the substance of this treatise by Egerton were wholly lost, and no longer available. But, as much as Egerton was regarded as "a man of great learning and godliness," it is quite easy to see this by this short treatise in and of itself. He has a vivid, masterful grasp of his matter, and dissects the doctrine of *hearing the word preached* in a catechistic manner through questions and thorough answers. Since God is speaking to us in the preached word by true ministers, that the minister's mouth is God's mouth in the act of preaching, one would do quite well to heed Rev. Egerton's application of Christ's exhortations to

---

[1] Harrison's works are limited to two, and both are powerhouse works. They are available from Puritan Publications.

hear what God is saying to us rightly, biblically, and for our good.

In Christ and His Grace,
C. Matthew McMahon, Ph.D.
From my study, February, 2019

Meet Stephen Egerton

Edited by C. Matthew McMahon, Ph.D.

Stephen Egerton (1555–1621) was a puritan divine, born in London about 1555. He became a member of St. Peter's College, Cambridge, and earned such a great reputation for learning that the only reason a fellowship was denied him was on account of the poverty of his college.

Egerton began his work to earn an M.A. degree in 1579, and on July 9, 1583 was incorporated at Oxford. He had already been ordained to the ministry and attached himself to the puritan party, being one of the leaders in the formation of the presbytery at Wandsworth, Surrey. This church has been described as the first Presbyterian church in England.

In 1584 he was suspended for refusing to subscribe to Whitgift's *articles*, but he does not appear to have remained long under criticism for this, for shortly afterwards, he was active in promoting the "Book of Discipline," and was one of those nominated by the puritan synod to superintend the proper performance of its articles.

During the imprisonment of Barrow and Greenwood in 1590 Egerton was sent by the Bishop of London to confer with them, and several letters passed between him and them; but later in the same year he himself was summoned, together with several other ministers, before the high commission, and was committed to the Fleet prison, where he remained about three years.

In 1598 he became minister of St. Anne's, Blackfriars, London. He was one of those chosen to present the millenary petition for the further reform of the church in 1603, and in May of the following year he introduced a petition to the lower house of convocation for the reformation of the prayer-book. He remained in his post at Blackfriars until his death, which took place about 1621, being assisted in his later years by William Gouge (1575-1653), who succeeded him. He was described by Dr. Nowell, in a letter, as a "man of great learning and godliness."

His works:

Egerton published several sermons, few of which remain. Chief among those of his works still available are

"A Brief Method of Catechising," first issued in 1594, which in 1644 reached a forty-fourth edition; and a translation created by Matthew Virel entitled "A Learned and Excellent Treatise containing all principal Grounds of the Christian Religion," the earliest edition of which now remaining is the fourth, published in 1597, and the latest the fourteenth in 1635. Egerton's preface to this book contains some well-chosen and sensible remarks on the choice of reading.

In addition to his own books he wrote introductions for several publications by his fellow-puritans, including Rogers, Pricke, Baine, and Nicholas Byfield.

[For further reading: Brook's *Lives of the Puritans*, ii. 289; Wood's *Athenæ Oxon.* ed. Bliss, i. 224; Strype's *Annals of the Reformation*, ii. pt. ii. 198, iii. pt. i. 691, iv. 553; Newcourt's *Report.* Eccl. Lond. i. 915; Wilson's *Hist. of Dissenting Churches*, i. 11.]

Original Title Page

THE BORING OF THE EAR,

Containing a plain and profitable Discourse by way of
Dialogue, concerning

1. Our preparation before Hearing.

2. Our demeanor in Hearing.

3. Our exercise after we have heard the Word of
God.

Written by that faithful and diligent Minister of God's
Word, Master Stephen Egerton, sometimes Preacher of
the Black-Friars in London.

ECCL. 5:1, "Look to thy feet when thou commest into the
House of God, and be readier to hear, then to offer the
sacrifice of fools."

LONDON
Printed by William Stansby,
1623.

To the Christian Reader

Christian Reader,

Though my own meditations have here ever shunned the common view of the world, contenting myself with the private approbation of my own charge. Yet, considering the general good that may accrue to the whole Church of Christ by these labors of my reverend kinsman, Master Stephen Egerton, I have ventured to commend them to God's church, being to it also entreated. I know, without my commendation, they will be worth your small cost in procuring, your little labor in perusing. For it is admirable to consider, that in these days of preaching and hearing, such faithful preaching, such frequent hearing, so many should yet be possessed as it were with a dumb devil,[2] and all our sermons to most men are but as sounding brass or a tinkling cymbal.[3] So we pipe, and no man dances, we mourn and no man weeps, we preach peace, but no man sorrows for

---

[2] "As they went out, behold, they brought to him a dumb man possessed with a devil." (Matt. 9:32).

[3] "Though I speak with the tongues of men and of angels, and have not charity, I am become as sounding brass, or a tinkling cymbal," (1 Cor. 13:1).

his sin.[4] May we not say of these, as David of the idols, "They have ears, but they hear not: noses have they, but they smell not: They have hands, but they handle not: feet have they, but they walk not: neither speak they through their throat," (Psa. 115:6-7). Or as our Savior translates that fearful threatening against despisers of his word, "Hearing they shall hear, and shall not understand, lest they hear with their ears, and understand with their hearts, and be converted and healed," (Isaiah 6:9-10; Matt. 13:14). So, to hear then, is to attend with the ear, to receive with the heart, to convert in life and conversation, otherwise our sinful souls can never be healed.

And therefore, this is the voice of the Spirit to the seven Churches of Asia, "He that hath ears to hear, let him hear what the Spirit saith unto the churches," (Rev. 2:17).

There are five sorts of ears that are not ears which hear. The first, is a dull ear, when a man is either drowsy, or careless, or ignorant.

The second, is a stopped ear, as the serpent stops his ear against the voice of the charmer. Such are our

---

[4] "And saying, We have piped unto you, and ye have not danced; we have mourned unto you, and ye have not lamented," (Matt. 11:17).

recusants, and secure people, that will not hear, that they should be thawed from their dregs, and so converted and saved.

The third, is a prejudicial or sinister ear. This man like Malchus has lost his right ear (Luke 10), and he comes as the Pharisee to Christ, to tempt the minister, to catch him in his talk, turning all his speech to the worst, because he hates or despises the person of the preacher. This man is like the spider that sucks poison out of the sweetest flowers.

The fourth, is the nice or itching ear[5] that must be clawed, that will hear nothing but novelties and dainties, that does not look so much to the goodness of the meat, as to the sweetness of the sauce. Surely this man must necessarily have a thin and pined soul, and he often meets with that which he does not understand. That is meat that he cannot digest, and so seldom or never profits by the Word of God.

The fifth is an adulterous ear, that will hear any but the voice of their own shepherds. You shall know them as the harlot is known, they are ever gadding to seek their new lovers. But, God shall one day discover their adultery to the shame of their persons, to the

---

[5] 2 Tim. 4:3; 2 Thess. 2:10; 2 Cor. 11:3.

disgrace of their profession, to the confusion of their faces. To such let me say, as Christ to the woman taken in adultery, "Go and sin no more," (John 10:8). Now all these have ears and they do not hear, and therefore, they have need to have the original word *Ephphata* pronounced to them as to the deaf man.[6] And for their better direction in this duty, this present treatise is of excellent use, being plain and familiar for its manner, and sound for its matter. It is grounded on many excellent exhortations, and rules in the Holy Scripture. By this, men may know how to hear with glory to God, honor to his ordinance, and profit to their own souls.

The necessity of this duty the Apostle proves where he in this way argues, "Faith commeth by hearing," (Romans 10:17), *etc.* Now without faith it is impossible to please God.

The neglect of, contempt of, or ignorance of this duty, is the cause of all profanes. If men would hear as they ought, this hearing would beget faith, and faith would bring forth all God's excellent graces accompanying salvation. The servant which bound himself to the perpetual service of his master because he

---

[6] "And looking up to heaven, he sighed, and saith unto him, Ephphatha, that is, Be opened," (Mark 7:34).

loved him was to be brought to the door of his house, and his Master, was to boar his ear with an awl.[7] Whoever he is that enters into God's service, he must have this mark, even an open ear, and it must *be bored* at the door of God's house, that he may be readier to hear, then to offer the sacrifice of fools.[8] The Hebrews say, it is the right ear that must *be bored.* Surely if men hear with a sinister ear, they do not express themselves as true servants of God. Whoever, therefore, has dedicated himself to the service of the Lord, let him express his obligation or indenture by his open ear to the Word of God. For Christ's sheep hear his voice, and his family does all his commands. God gives to everyone that he receives into his service, this jewel to hang in his ear, namely, to hear with attention and reverence.

1. Whatever God speaks.

2. Whenever he speaks.

3. By whomever he speaks.

The next punishment to death by our National law, is losing an ear. And certainly whose ears or hearing

---

[7] "Then his master shall bring him unto the judges; he shall also bring him to the door, or unto the door post; and his master shall bore his ear through with an aul; and he shall serve him for ever," (Exod. 21:6).

[8] "Keep thy foot when thou goest to the house of God, and be more ready to hear, than to give the sacrifice of fools: for they consider not that they do evil," (Eccl. 5:1).

God have suffered to be taken away, they are in a dangerous or desperate case, because the Word is the savor of life to the right hearer, and the savor of death to him that does not hear as he ought.[9] Now that you may hear with your ears, and understand with your hearts, and be converted from your evil ways, and be healed of all your sins, use this short and easy receipt. As you find it effectual, return all the glory to God, esteem him who has presented it to your view, and use it as one that has good will to Zion. Moan for the deafness of the daughter of his people, and ever pray that this word Ephphatha[10] may be by the Spirit of the Lord effectually pronounced to all those who desire to hear the glad tidings of the Gospel of Jesus Christ. To whom, with the Father and the Holy Ghost, be all honor and praise, and obedience yielded, now and for ever, AMEN.

Yours in the Lord Jesus to be commanded.

RICHARD CROOKE

---

[9] "To the one we are the savour of death unto death; and to the other the savour of life unto life. And who is sufficient for these things?" (2 Cor. 2:16).

[10] *Ephphatha* "be open," (Mark. 7:34).

To the Reader

Of all the senses, none is more needful, or useful, than hearing. Of all the objects of hearing, none are to be compared to hearing the Word of God. To be taught, then, *how* to hear the Word of God, must necessarily be a lesson worth learning. In this treatise that doctrine is taught. The author[11] who first indited it (being a man by long practice and much experience, acquainted with the *boring of the ear*) the matter contained in it (being a means which is sanctified by God to bring us to life and happiness)[12] and the manner of unfolding that matter (being distinct and perspicuous) does in a special manner commend it to you. Come and read. Read and judge.

WILLIAM GOUGE.

---

[11] Master Stephen Egerton of Black-fryers, London.

[12] "Incline your ear, and come unto me: hear, and your soul shall live; and I will make an everlasting covenant with you, even the sure mercies of David," (Isa. 55:3). "But he said, Yea rather, blessed are they that hear the word of God, and keep it," (Luke 11:28).

CHAPTER 1:
Taking Heed to the Preached Word

"Take heed therefore how ye hear: for whosoever hath, to him shall be given; and whosoever hath not, from him shall be taken even that which he seemeth to have," (Luke 8:18).

Question. Is it a hard matter to hear the Word of God preached heedfully, and with fruit?

Answer. Yes, very much so. Otherwise, our Savior Jesus Christ would never have exhorted and persuaded his hearers to perform this duty by so many arguments.

Question. What arguments does he use?

Answer. In this parable he uses diverse reasons. First, because it is a very rare and dainty thing to hear the Word profitably, seeing among so many thousands that flock together, scarcely the fourth part of them reap any profit. Many times, preachers do not call men to account. And yet though parents, pastors, masters, *etc.* neglect us, yet God will call us to account. It will appear one day to come on all those who have a conscience to this duty, and those who not.

Question. What other reasons may be gathered out of the words of Christ, to prove the profit, necessity, and difficulty of hearing?

Answer. There are diverse answers to this. First, to be a good and fruitful hearer is a special gift of God, and peculiar to the elect, "My sheep hear my voice," (John 10:27). And again, "he that is of God, heareth God's Word," (John 8:47). And Christ showing the reason why his disciples profited rather than others, says, "And he said, Unto you it is given to know the mysteries of the kingdom of God: but to others in parables; that seeing they might not see, and hearing they might not understand," (Luke 8:10). And there are many other Scriptures to the same purpose, as when true faith is called the faith of the elect.[13]

Secondly, in respect of the excellency of the Word, which is called the Word of the Kingdom, both in respect of the subject, and also of the effect. To the same purpose it is called, "The power of God to salvation to everyone that believeth," (Romans 1:16). "The Word of grace, and faith," (Acts 26:32 and Titus 2:11). Seeing then, it is the word of the Kingdom, yes, of such a

---

[13] "Paul, a servant of God, and an apostle of Jesus Christ, according to the faith of God's elect, and the acknowledging of the truth which is after godliness," (Titus 1:1).

Kingdom, with what attention, resolution, and heedfulness ought we to hear it? Jehu and his companions counted the prophet a mad fellow. Yet, when he brought him tidings of a Kingdom, he was glad to hear it, and willing to embrace it.[14]

Thirdly, to the same purpose (which may be another reason) it is called *seed*, yes, immortal seed,[15] on which the Apostle makes the same conclusion in effect,[16] that Christ does here in this place saying, "Wherefore, my dear brethren, let every man be swift to hear, and slow to wrath," *etc.* The wrath of man does not work the righteousness of God. So, the minister is called the Lord's Sower (Matthew 13), or Husbandman, and the people his husbandry, and the time of preaching, the

---

[14] "And he arose, and went into the house; and he poured the oil on his head, and said unto him, Thus saith the LORD God of Israel, I have anointed thee king over the people of the LORD, even over Israel. And thou shalt smite the house of Ahab thy master, that I may avenge the blood of my servants the prophets, and the blood of all the servants of the LORD, at the hand of Jezebel. For the whole house of Ahab shall perish: and I will cut off from Ahab him that pisseth against the wall, and him that is shut up and left in Israel," (2 Kings 9:6-8).

[15] "Being born again, not of corruptible seed, but of incorruptible, by the word of God, which liveth and abideth for ever," (1 Peter 1:23).

[16] "Every good gift and every perfect gift is from above, and cometh down from the Father of lights, with whom is no variableness, neither shadow of turning. Of his own will begat he us with the word of truth, that we should be a kind of firstfruits of his creatures. Wherefore, my beloved brethren, let every man be swift to hear, slow to speak, slow to wrath: For the wrath of man worketh not the righteousness of God," (James 1:17-20).

time of sowing or the seed time. Shall we then cast away ourselves, and cause the Lord to lose both his labor and cost upon us?

Fourthly, in which (being a fourth reason) we are to be more vigilant, because Satan, like a ravening fowl follows us right at our heals, *etc.* as at all times, and in all holy duties. He does this especially in hearing the word. Let us remember that we do not (as the Apostle says) "wrestle against flesh and blood, but against principalities, and powers," (Eph. 6:12), *etc.*

Fifthly, a fifth reason (likewise arising from here) may be this: it is a rare and singular grace which few attain to hear the Word of God effectively. Scarcely one in four do this; yes, rather scarcely one of forty that hears heedfully with fruit, reverent attention,[17] *etc.* Plain experience proves as much, let ministers examine their people, parents their children, masters their servants, *etc.* and it will plainly appear how slenderly they have heard. Yes, let every man examine his own heart, and call himself to account concerning those things which have been delivered in the public congregation, and his

---

[17] "Thou shalt not muzzle the ox when he treadeth out the corn," (Deut. 25:4). "And a certain woman named Lydia, a seller of purple, of the city of Thyatira, which worshipped God, heard us: whose heart the Lord opened, that she attended unto the things which were spoken of Paul," (Acts 16:14).

conscience will tell him, what a heedless and unprofitable hearer he has been.[18]

Sixthly and lastly, the great gain and increase promised to careful hearers, ought to encourage us. Christ says, ""Take heed therefore how ye hear: for whosoever hath, to him shall be given; and whosoever hath not, from him shall be taken even that which he seemeth to have," (Luke 8:18). This is something rare and excellent, profitable and difficult; for the fat heart, dull ears, heavy head and drowsy eyes get nothing good from it. Let no man think with himself, "I will now sit down and take my place, and sit down at ease, and hear at pleasure," but rather let him in this way think, "I will go now to an exercise indeed (although some scorn, and others foolishly impropriate the word) I must now fight with Satan and mine own corruption, *etc.*[19]

Question. Seeing then it is such a necessary duty, so profitable, rare, excellent and difficult to hear well,

---

[18] "And he shewed me Joshua the high priest standing before the angel of the LORD, and Satan standing at his right hand to resist him," (Zech. 3:1). "Be sober, be vigilant; because your adversary the devil, as a roaring lion, walketh about, seeking whom he may devour:" (1 Peter 5:8).

[19] "For bodily exercise profiteth little: but godliness is profitable unto all things, having promise of the life that now is, and of that which is to come," (1 Tim. 4:8).

what things are chiefly to be respected to the end that we may hear as we ought?

Answer. To the end that we may hear as we ought, we are to consider, first, what is to be done before the sermon. Secondly, what is to be done while the sermon is being preached, and lastly, what is to be done after the sermon.

CHAPTER 2:
Duties Before Hearing the Sermon

Question. What is the general duty of hearers before the sermon is given?

Answer. Their duty is, with great care and conscience to prepare and sanctify themselves.

Question. How is that proved?

Answer. First, by plain and evident precepts and testimonies of Scripture, both in the Old and New Testament. Solomon says, "Look well to thy feet when thou goest to the house of God, so as thou mayst be prepared to hear," (Eccl. 5:1), that is, to obey and believe the word of God preached in his Temple. This is as if he should say, you must look to be more careful to offer up yourself to God by giving him an obedient heart and ear, *then* bring calves, goats, *etc.* For without a believing and obedient heart, as the manner of hypocrites and worldlings is, James 1:21-22 says, "Lay apart all filthiness, and superfluity of maliciousness, and receive with meekness the word that is grafted in you, which is able to save your souls."

Secondly, the practice of God's faithful people, both before the Law, (Gen. 35:2; Job 1:5). And at the giving of the Law, (Exod. 19:10), and likewise after the Law, (1 Sam. 16:5; 2 Chronicles 15:12 and 2 Chron. 29:5; Joel 2:15-16).

Thirdly, you must consider the glorious majesty of God before whom we come to worship in hearing the Word preached.

Fourthly, the excellency of these heavenly things which in this holy meeting are propounded unto us.[20]

Fifthly, our own insufficiency. "Not that we are sufficient of ourselves to think any thing as of ourselves; but our sufficiency is of God," (2 Cor. 3:5).

Sixthly, the pollution and uncleanness both of our hearts and lives. In this respect we ought to listen to the saying of the holy Apostle in James 4:8, "Cleanse your hands ye sinners, and purge your hearts ye double minded men, and so draw near to God, and he will draw near to you."

Seventhly, (this may be referred back also to the fifth reason) if the heathen did so highly esteem their devilish mysteries that they used to say, "Be gone, be

---

[20] "But as it is written, Eye hath not seen, nor ear heard, neither have entered into the heart of man, the things which God hath prepared for them that love him," (1 Cor. 2:9). "And without controversy great is the mystery of godliness: God was manifest in the flesh, justified in the Spirit, seen of angels, preached unto the Gentiles, believed on in the world, received up into glory," (1 Tim. 3:16). (*cf.* 1 Peter 1).

gone far from here all ye profane ones," and when the Pharisees taught, "Touch no unclean thing with unwashen hands," then how much more ought we to think in this way of the great and holy Mystery of Godliness, and accordingly prepare ourselves to be partakers of it?

Question. You have showed me generally what is to be done of all men before the sermon, now tell what is to be done more particularly.

Answer. First, they must carefully avoid surfeiting and drunkenness, and disorder in diet. They ought to use great moderation and sobriety, especially overnight, and in the morning before they resort to the public assemblies. Christ says, ""And take heed to yourselves, lest at any time your hearts be overcharged with surfeiting, and drunkenness, and cares of this life, and so that day come upon you unawares," (Luke 21:34). If at all times we must take heed, how much more should we at this time of coming to the Word of God? For "wine is a mocker," Solomon says, "and strong drink is raging," (Proverbs 20:1). And as the prophet says, "Wine and strong drink take away the heart." And Isaiah says, "Woe be to them that rise early to follow drunkenness," *etc.* then he giveth the reason, saying in Isaiah 11:24,

"They regard not the Lord's work, but despise the Law of the Lord of Hosts." Where the Apostle says, "Be not filled with wine, wherein is excess, but be ye filled with the Spirit," (Eph. 4:17-18). He shows that fullness is an enemy to spiritual graces. So, being heedful and profitable in hearing the word is one and the same thing.

Question. What is the next particular hinderance to be avoided when we are to go to the House of God?

Answer. Excessive care and minding of earthly things, which are reckoned up as those special thorns that choke the seed of the Word of God, that it cannot bring forth fruit *in due season* (Luke 8:14). Therefore, when we go to hear a sermon, we must endeavor by all means to empty and disburden ourselves of all such thoughts, casting them from us as Thales did his goods, choosing rather to drown them, then let them drown us by trouble and distraction.

Question. What is the third particular hinderance?

Answer. A conceit and overweening of some singular knowledge and reliance on books and reading. Books often come with such a prejudice as will not suffer us to reap any profit by the Word preached because we are taken up with all their teachings instead.

Question. What are the most convenient remedies for the removing this evil?

Answer. To this purpose we are first to call to mind, that the preaching of the Gospel is the power of God to salvation, not to the simple and unlearned only, but even to *everyone that believes,* (Romans 1:16).

Secondly, that these mysteries are of that nature and so disposed by the providence of God, that they are often revealed to babes in knowledge and learning, when they are hid from the wise and prudent.[21] Therefore, the more witty, learned, and quick of conceit that men are, the more need they have to resort to the House of God with fear and trembling.

Thirdly, the examples of God's faithful servants. David was not only a wise, and witty Prince, but also a holy Prophet, and a man known for his piety and other spiritual graces which are most dear and acceptable to God. Yet, who was more desirous and forward to hear the Word of God then he was?[22] Aquila and Priscilla had

---

[21] "At that time Jesus answered and said, I thank thee, O Father, Lord of heaven and earth, because thou hast hid these things from the wise and prudent, and hast revealed them unto babes," (Matt. 11:25).

[22] Psa. 42, 84, 122.

better knowledge then Apollos himself even as an eloquent preacher, yet they did not disdain to hear him.[23] Nor did Apollos disdain to hear them, though he was more learned in other things.

Lastly, the public assemblies of the church have a more singular promises of God's present grace and blessings, as may appear by various places of Scripture.[24]

Question. What is the fourth hinderance?

Answer. A partial, or rather schismatic respect of persons, such as was in the church of Corinth, where some extolled one, and some another, some Paul, some Apollos?[25]

Question. Where does this proceed this respect of persons?

Answer. It proceeds originally from the hearers, either from the ignorance of their minds, or from the corruption of their hearts. Occasionally it comes from the teachers, in respect of the diversity of their gifts, and manner of handling of the Scriptures.

---

[23] "And he began to speak boldly in the synagogue: whom when Aquila and Priscilla had heard, they took him unto them, and expounded unto him the way of God more perfectly," (Acts 18:26).
[24] Psa. 29:9; Joel 2:22; Rom. 10:13-15; Matt. 15:19-20.
[25] "For ye are yet carnal: for whereas there is among you envying, and strife, and divisions, are ye not carnal, and walk as men? For while one saith, I am of Paul; and another, I am of Apollos; are ye not carnal?" (1 Cor. 3:3-4).

Question. How are men hindered by their own ignorance, and corruption?

Answer. When for lack of Judgment and sanctimony, they prefer such who speak pleasing things, and tickle their ears with eloquent terms, pleasant stories, and witty jokes, and cannot bear to listen with those that speak the words of truth and soberness.[26] This is the same thing the Apostle says when wholesome doctrine becomes neglected. Especially, if they plainly and roundly lay their sins before them. It is here that Ahab could not endure Micaiah.[27] This made Felix cut off Paul in the midst of his speech (Acts 24:25) and put him off until another time. Here sprang the imprisonment of John Baptist by Herod (Matthew 14).

Question. What are the remedies against this hinderance?

Answer. For a remedy against this evil we are to consider, first, that such partial respect of God's

---

[26] Acts 26; Titus 2:1.

[27] "And Jehoshaphat said, Is there not here a prophet of the LORD besides, that we might enquire of him? And the king of Israel said unto Jehoshaphat, There is yet one man, Micaiah the son of Imlah, by whom we may enquire of the LORD: but I hate him; for he doth not prophesy good concerning me, but evil. And Jehoshaphat said, Let not the king say so," (1 Kings 22:7-8).

ministers argues a carnal and a fleshly mind,[28] and shows that we are babes and children in our Christian walk.

Secondly, that by this partiality we give to man more than his due and take from Christ that which of right belongs to him as appears in 1 Cor. 11:12-13 and 3:1-5.

Thirdly, that this diversity and inequality of gifts is not given for the renting and destroying, but for the building, and the beautifying of the Church of Christ, even as the diversity, and variety of flowers in the same Garden differing in color, smell, taste and virtue, bring no confusion nor deformity. They deck the ground, and serve for the use and comfort of man. And the manifold variety of strings and instruments make the sweetest harmony in an orchestra.

Fourthly, remember that no minister excels in all gifts. And true ministers have but some special gifts and graces of edification. One is more profound in knowledge to inform the judgement of a man. Another is more powerful in preaching for inflaming the affections. One is more fit to humble and beat down the proud, careless and conceited person. Another is used to

---

[28] "For while one saith, I am of Paul; and another, I am of Apollos; are ye not carnal?" (1 Cor. 3:4).

comfort and raise up penitent sinners. One has a special grace to work godly sorrow, another to procure supernatural comfort and joy.[29]

Fifthly, remember that the contempt of any true minister is the contempt of God himself.

Sixthly, let it be kept in mind that Christian hearers look rather to the pith and substance of the matter, then to the enticements and paintings of the speech.

Question. What is the fifth hinderance to be removed before the Sermon?

Answer. The fifth (which may be referred to the former) is a certain hatred of the ministers and loathing of the ministry, such as was in the Jews, which made them to fret at Christ, and stop their ears against him.[30]

Question. From where arises this hatred of ministers, and the ministry?

Answer. Sometimes from the personal behavior of the minister himself, but commonly from the matter which he delivers, by which the errors of their judgment,

---

[29] Matt. 11:16-17 and Luke 10:16.

[30] "But he, being full of the Holy Ghost, looked up stedfastly into heaven, and saw the glory of God, and Jesus standing on the right hand of God, And said, Behold, I see the heavens opened, and the Son of man standing on the right hand of God. Then they cried out with a loud voice, and stopped their ears, and ran upon him with one accord," (Acts 7:55-57).

and corruptions of their hearts and lives, are laid open, and reproved. This made Ahab to count Elijah as his enemy, and to hate Micaiah.[31] And Herod in Matthew 14 did the same and committed John the Baptist to prison, as before you heard.

Question. What are the remedies against this hinderance?

Answer. Let such haters and despisers of the ministry consider *that:*

First, they do not despise man but God,[32] for all true ministers are the Lord's ambassadors.

Secondly, they greatly prejudice themselves, in neglecting, much more in loathing the means of their comfort and salvation.[33] Men willingly bow to the tree that yielded them a shadow. How much more, then, ought they to submit themselves to the grace of God, that brings salvation, *etc.*[34]

Thirdly, it is a point of godly wisdom to distinguish between the people and the office, and not to deprive ourselves of the fruit of the Word for the fault

---

[31] 1 Kings 18; 1 Kings 22.

[32] 1 Sam. 8:7; Luke 10:16; John 13:22; 1 Thess. 4:8; 2 Cor. 5:10ff.

[33] "For I am not ashamed of the gospel of Christ: for it is the power of God unto salvation to every one that believeth; to the Jew first, and also to the Greek," (Romans 1:16).

[34] "For the grace of God that bringeth salvation hath appeared to all men," (Titus 2:11).

of the teacher. In outward things men are wise. No man will refuse a good workman for some personal sin. He that decides to build a house will not think the worse of the work because the carpenter is wicked. He that is hungry will not refuse his food because the cook that made it is a drunkard. Why then should we distaste the food of our souls by reason of the sin of the one that distributes it to us? Would any man refuse the prince's gift because the messenger that brings it is a Machiavellian,[35] *etc.*

Question. What else makes men hate the ministry?

Answer. Besides that natural corruption which is common to all, there is in many a satiety, and fulness, now (as Solomon says), "He that is full despiseth a honeycomb; but to him that is hungry, far bitterer things are sweet," (Proverbs 27:7).

Secondly, that rebukes and threatenings, though they are tedious to the flesh, yet they are wholesome medicines to the soul, and strong defenses against Satan, *etc.* And therefore, they should pray with David, "Let the righteous smite me, (Psalm 141) *etc.* and praise God

---

[35] A cunning, scheming, and unscrupulous person especially in politics.

because the righteous has struck them, as men do for the surgeon when he has healed them even by a painful searching and incision.

Question. What is the sixth impediment to be striven against?

Answer. The length of the way to church, foulness of the weather, weakness in the parties, lack of means to carry them, *etc.*

Question. What encouragements have we to overcome these impediments?

Answer. We have, First, the Law that God laid on the Israelites, to appear before the Lord three times every year, and that with their whole Family, and not empty handed, to the place appointed by God, which must necessarily be far off from a number of their dwellings.[36]

Secondly, The promise of saving them from their enemies while they were so employed.[37] Now considering that God is the God of the Gentiles, as well as of the Jews, it cannot be but that the Gentiles are proportionably bound both to obey the commandments,

---

[36] Exod. 23:17; Deut. 12:11-12.
[37] Exod. 34:24.

and believe the promises given to the Jews. There are some particular differences between them.[38]

Thirdly, The practice and examples of the godly in former times both of the Old and New Testament.

Fourthly, by comparison; if men take such journeys, and make such ventures, for their bodily provision, how much more ought they to do for the good of their souls?

Question. What do you say to the aged, sick, and such as have young children?

Answer. Touching all these in general, care must be had.

First, that they do not make a necessity where none is.

Secondly, they must endeavor though they cannot go all at once, nor every Lord's Day, yet that they go as often as they can by turns, each one in his course.

Thirdly, they must be more careful to ask questions, and to desire repetition of the sermon, of those that were there.

Fourthly, they must keep no more at home with them, then of necessity that they need, and such they may lawfully keep to attend on themselves being aged,

---

[38] See 2 Kings 4:23; Luke 2:42; Acts 2:5, 8:27; Matt. 5:32.

sickly, impotent, having children, *etc.,* for in this the saying of the Holy Ghost may be remembered, "Obedience is better than sacrifice," (1 Sam. 15:22). And again, "I will have mercy and not sacrifice," (Hosea 6:6).

Question. What is the seventh impediment?

Answer. The last and greatest impediment (which comprehends in effect all the former ones,) is carnal security, impenitency, worldliness, uncleanness of life, *etc.,* which things either withdraw men altogether from hearing, or else make them hear with a deaf ear, and a dead heart, *etc.*

Question. What is the remedy for this?

Answer. True and unfeigned repentance, and especially that one fruit and companion of repentance which may be a care and desire both to know, believe and obey the Lord, speaking to us in his holy Word. For it cannot be but by the blessing of God they must necessarily profit that go to public assemblies, as the soldiers, publicans and people came to John the Baptist in Luke 3:10-12, saying, "What shall we do?" Especially when they are touched in their heart with the feeling of their sin, and the terror of God's judgment hanging over their heads for the same, as the people were. In Acts 2:37 this happened to the jailer.[39]

Question. You have showed me what impediments are to be avoided. Now, let me know what duties are to be performed concerning this point.

Answer. First, let such as are the governors of families bring as near as may be their whole family with them, excepting only such as are apparently like to be hurt, by reason of their sickness, or to disturb the congregation by reason of their unruliness, that they may show the zeal of faithful Joshua, saying, "I and my household will serve the Lord," (Josh 24:15), and with holy Esther, "I and my maids will do likewise," (Esther 4:16), that is, fast and pray.

Question. What is the second duty?

Answer. Such as have neighbors must endeavor to encourage and quicken them to join in company, and to go together to the house of God, saying, as it is in Isaiah, "O house of Jacob come, and let us walk in the light of the Lord,"[40] and with the woman of Samaria, "Come and see a man," in John 4, *etc.* So let us say, "Come and hear a man," *etc.* The performance of this holy duty

---

[39] Acts 2:37 and 16:30.
[40] Isaiah 2:5 and Hosea 6:1.

made David glad in his very heart (Psalm 12). In this way, Philip and Andrew invited Nathaniel and Simon (John 1:45) to come to Christ whom they had found before.

Question. What is the third duty?

Answer. As we go to the place of public assemblies, we must be occupied and exercise our minds with religious and holy meditations, not suffering our own lusts and cares of the world, and Satan with them to creep in and enter with us into the house of God.

Question. What are those holy meditations which we ought to have?

Answer. Diverse, as has been partly showed before, as namely, first, consider who it is before whom we come, namely, before him who is King of Kings, *etc.*

Secondly, what is the thing we come to,[41] namely, a supernatural banquet and heavenly table for the refreshing and satisfying of our faint and hungry souls, which will work a brisk and cheerful readiness, as the former will humility. We see how it takes up men's hearts if they go to speak with an earthly king, and to hear him speak with them and bid them to his table.[42] How much more, when we go before the King of heaven

---

[41] 1 Tim. 6:15; Prov. 9:1, *etc.*
[42] "When thou sittest to eat with a ruler, consider diligently what is before thee," (Prov. 23:1).

and earth to speak to him by prayer, and to hear him by preaching, and by both of these as also by the sacraments to feast and feed with him?

Thirdly, we must remember more particularly, the fruit of God's Word, and its efficacy, in that it is called, the Kingdom of Heaven,[43] the means to keep us from hell,[44] the treasury of eternal life, a sure word of prophesy, compared to a light that shines in a dark place, and is not only food to nourish us, but also seed to beget us, being able to save our souls.[45] It is that which will support us, and quicken us in our greatest troubles, being the very joy of our hearts.[46]

Question. What is the fourth duty?

Answer. Fourthly, we are to read and meditate in private with others if we may do so fitly, and by ourselves on that place of Scripture that is to be handled

---

[43] "And saying, Repent ye: for the kingdom of heaven is at hand," (Matt. 3:2).

[44] Luke 16:29; John 5:39; 1 Peter 1:19.

[45] James 1:18; 1 Peter 1:23; James 1:21; Psa. 119:53, 92.

[46] "O LORD, thou knowest: remember me, and visit me, and revenge me of my persecutors; take me not away in thy longsuffering: know that for thy sake I have suffered rebuke. Thy words were found, and I did eat them; and thy word was unto me the joy and rejoicing of mine heart: for I am called by thy name, O LORD God of hosts. I sat not in the assembly of the mockers, nor rejoiced; I sat alone because of thy hand: for thou hast filled me with indignation. Why is my pain perpetual, and my wound incurable, which refuseth to be healed? wilt thou be altogether unto me as a liar, and as waters that fail?" (Jer. 15:15-18).

in the public assembly. For if a godly man ought to meditate "day and night" (Psalm 1:2), in the Law of the Lord, how can he be negligent on the day of the Lord in thinking of that Scripture which is to be handled in the house of the Lord? And if the whole doctrine of the Gospel ought to dwell plentifully in us always (Col. 3:16), how can we but possess ourselves of that part of the Gospel or Word of God, which we now go to feed our souls with? Moreover, a Christian shall better remember the matter which is delivered, when he has thought of its ground before. And he can also discern more clearly the grace, and power of the public ministry so far exceeding his private meditations, or, otherwise the weakness of the minister if he lacks either that gift that he should have or be negligent in that study and preparation which he ought to use.[47]

Question. What is the fifth duty to be used of the hearers before the sermon?

Answer. He must pour forth faithful and hearty prayer, first for himself, that God will enlighten his mind, confirm his memory, reform his Will, soften his heart, purify his conscience, that he may grow in the

---

[47] "Withal praying also for us, that God would open unto us a door of utterance, to speak the mystery of Christ, for which I am also in bonds," (Col. 4:3).

knowledge of his heavenly doctrine, lay hold of it by a true faith, and turn the same into the daily, and wholesome exercises of prayer and repentance. In this he imitates the prophet David, and the Apostles.[48]

Secondly, for the people that shall join with him, especially those of his own family. For if there are people that are worse than infidels, as to not make bodily provision for their Families, neither can they be Christians that neglect this part of provision for their souls.

Thirdly, for their ministers. If Paul being so excellent an Apostle, needed the prayers of the Ephesians (6:19), much more do the ordinary pastors, and teachers of the Church need those prayers as well.

Question. Why else is prayer necessary?

Answer. Because, first, only God gives wisdom (Proverbs 2:6), and out of his mouth comes knowledge and understanding.

Secondly, flesh and blood do not reveal those things to us, but God our heavenly Father (Matthew 16:17).

Thirdly, the natural man does not perceive the things which belong to the Spirit of God, (1 Cor. 2:16).

---

[48] Psa. 25:4-5, 119:18, 33; Luke 17:5.

CHAPTER 3:
Duties While Hearing the Sermon

Question. You have showed me what is to be done before the sermon, now tell me what is the hearer's duty in the sermon while it is being preached?

Answer. First, let such as are able to read, bring with them to the public Assemblies the holy Bible, to the end that they may not only join with the church in singing of psalms, but also readily turn to the principal places of Scriptures that are read, expounded, and repeated by the minister. By these means they shall greatly further both their attention and memory, having the help, not only of their ear in hearing, but also of their eye in perusing those scriptures that are alleged. They can see whether they are truly alleged or not in the preaching. By this means also the minister shall be made more careful to take heed, that he does not, except on very good ground, swerve from the words of the common translation. If this had been observed, the Novatian Heretic of whom Socrates speaks about in the *Ecclesiasticall Storie,*[49] would not dare have added those words to the text which he did, saying, "Cursed is every

---

[49] Lib. 7. cap. 5

one that keepeth the Passover (Luke 22:1) without unleavened bread." Neither would it have been erroneous of whom Augustine speaks *Epistola nona ad Hicon*, have so unadvisedly made that hurry among the people, by reading a word in the Prophesy of Jonah, in some other way than it was in their Bibles.

Question. Which is the second duty?

Answer. Every hearer must endeavor earnestly to be present at the whole sermon, from the beginning to the end, both coming before the first prayer begins, and not departing until the blessing is pronounced.[50] Judas left the assembly of Christ and the other Apostles before the action was ended, and the psalm sung. This was counted such a great fault in former times, that the Council of Carthage appointed that the one that went out of the congregation while the minister was speaking, was to be excommunicated.

Question. What is the third?

Answer. Sleep, talk, and speech with other men, curiosity in looking about, and reading of other books, *etc.* during the time of the sermons must be avoided.

---

[50] "And the first day of unleavened bread, when they killed the passover, his disciples said unto him, Where wilt thou that we go and prepare that thou mayest eat the passover?" (Mark 14:12). They considered this ahead of time.

Question. Why should men not sleep at sermons?

Answer. For diverse reasons. First, it is a breach of the third commandment, or taking God's name in vain by neglect, and abuse of God's holy Ordinance.

Secondly, it is an enemy to that attention, and heedfulness in hearing which is required of us.

Thirdly, if such a judgement befell him that slept in the night, and that at an exceeding long sermon (Acts 20:9-10), what are we to say of those that sleep in the day at a sermon that is only an hour long?

Fourthly, it is a thing of evil report and example.

Question. How shall they prevent it, that by reason of watching, early rising, age, or other infirmities can hardly avoid it?

Answer. They must seek by all means to resist it, praying and groaning in spirit, standing up, using the pen if they can write, craving the help of such as sit near them, *etc.*

Question. What say you to talking, curious gazing, and gaping about, *etc?*

Answer. They are condemned by all the same reasons that sleeping is, and that so much more, because sleep is such a natural infirmity, that it may suddenly and unawares steal on a good and godly man, who has often resolved with his own heart never to give place to it. Where, any man that has but a spark of grace and modesty, may with a little striving, refrain from talking, and looking about, and therefore, it argues a far greater profaneness and impudence then the other.

Question. But may not a man read some good book of divinity during the sermon?

Answer. No, not even the Bible itself, except it is in the places that are pointed to by the minister, for we are to give attendance to the things that are spoken (Acts 8:6). Besides, it carries with it a kind of contempt both of the minister, and ministry, and a secret condemning of those that attend preaching.

Question. What is the fourth duty of hearers?

Answer. He must mark the whole sermon from its beginning to the end, and ponder as well one part of the sentence, as another. He must not take things in halves, or by snatches, as some people do. This breeds great inconvenience. For it comes here that things spoken comparatively are wrested out of place, as if they were spoken simply. It is here that the proposition of a similitude is marked, and the application neglected, with diverse other inconveniences. And because people only hear half a truth, or half a sermon, or part of it, from this arises errors, scoffings, cavilings, *etc.*

Question. What is the fifth duty?

Answer. The fifth duty which may be referred to the impediments, is to come with a free mind not possessed with any prejudice or fore-stalled opinion, but in trying the spirits of the ministers of God to hold fast that which is good (1 John 4:5). For as colored glasses makes all things of the same color, so a prejudicated opinion makes all things sound in a way that a person imagines. This made even the best hearers of our Savior Christ, sometimes not understand him when he spoke most plainly to them of his sufferings. They were possessed with a preconceived opinion of a worldly Kingdom (Luke 18:31-32). Let us therefore when we go to the house of God, look to our feet, that is, not to our corrupt affections alone (Eccl. 5:1), but also to our prejudicated opinions and conceits.

Question. What is the sixth duty?

Answer. Sixthly, we must not be present with a mind peremptorily to determine, according to our own imagination, or to toss, and sift things to and fro, as we wish, as if we were masters rather than scholars, teachers, rather than hearers, judges and censurers of others rather than learners. For there is nothing that can be so truly and plainly spoken, but pride and malice may pervert it.[51] Therefore, let us lay aside all sinister conceits of our own knowledge, wit, and learning, all contempt and hatred of the minister's person, vain glory, self-love, *etc.,* which does not make men think anything right and good but that which comes from themselves. Neither let us count it a goodly thing to dissent from others.

Question. Does not the Apostle desire us to try the spirits, and judge of those things which the Prophets speak? (1 Cor. 14:19).

Answer. Yes, but it is not his meaning that men should of envy, vain-glory, *etc.* subject the sermons they hear to their own proud and malicious minds. But only with wisdom, charity and sobriety to consider whether the things delivered by the preachers and ministers agree with the rule of God's Word, and the soundness of Christian faith. Further, that will come to pass if men give place to their own conceits, which is said in the common proverb, "So many men, so many minds," *Quot homines, tot sententiae.*

---

[51] "And it came to pass, as he went into the house of one of the chief Pharisees to eat bread on the sabbath day, that they watched him," (Luke 14:1).

Question. What is the seventh duty of hearers in the preaching of a sermon?

Answer. Not to be rashly discouraged or distasted with those things which at first may seem difficult and hard. But rather to use more diligence, and attention to find them out.

Question. Why so?

Answer. Because, first, we must remember that the natural man (1 Cor. 2:14) does not easily conceive heavenly things.

Secondly, it is the will of God by this means to humble us, and to abate the ambitious conceits of our own will, and to stir up our dullness in prayer, meditation, and study, that the LORD would enlighten the eyes of our understanding, and to repair to the ministers of God's Word.

Thirdly, men do readily despise these things which are over easy and familiar at first, and through loathsomeness grow faint, lazy, and without desire.

Question. What is the eighth duty?

Answer. To understand, and mark the method and order of the preacher.

Question. Why so?

Answer. Because it is a great help to the memory and serves as the star in the sky of the sailor, and as a thread or line without which he shall be entangled as in entering into a maze.

Question. How shall the hearer attain to this?

Answer. This stands partly in the preacher himself, who must keep a good order, otherwise it will be hard to follow him step by step. Secondly, in the hearers themselves three things are required for the help of their memory in the time of the hearer.

First, diligent marking, not suffering their minds to stray abroad about other matters.

Secondly, looking thoroughly to the text, to see how the doctrines, exhortations, *etc.,* are raised.

Thirdly, to observe to what point of the catechism, or head of religion, everything is to be referred.

Question. What is the ninth duty of the hearer in the preaching of the sermon?

Answer. To apply that which is preached, to himself, and so to turn it to its wholesome use, and spiritual nourishment of his soul.

Question. Why so?

Answer. Because the end of hearing is not chiefly to know and understand, but rather to believe, practice, and obey that which is taught.[52]

Question. How shall the hearer apply that which is taught, to himself?

Answer. If it is a promise, by believing, and embracing. If a threatening, by believing, and fearing it. If a precept or duty laid forth, by believing, and endeavoring to practice it. If a prohibition from a sin laid out and reproved, by believing, repenting, and shunning it. Finally, in every point that is delivered, they put on themselves the same affection and feeling that is in their godly teacher.

Question. What is the tenth duty?

Answer. Not to fret and become weary and impatient, though the minister be somewhat longer then the ordinary time.

Question. Ought not the Minister to keep himself within the compass of his hour?

Answer. Yes, he ought to endeavor it as near as he can.

Question. Has not the hearer just cause to be offended?

---

[52] Matt. 7:21; Luke 11:28, 12:47; John 13:7; Rom. 2:13; James 2:1ff.

Answer. No, for there may be diverse reasons which may justly move a godly minister to go beyond his hour, and therefore, the hearer ought quietly and patiently to continue to the end of the sermon.

Question. What are those?

Answer. They are diverse: as first, the fruitfulness of the text which he handles.

Secondly, the necessity and profit of it for the time and persons that be present.

Thirdly, lack of opportunity to handle the same text another time. These, and other considerations may give the minister just occasion to be longer than ordinary, and therefore, the hearer ought not to chafe, and fume, though he exceeds his time a little.

Question. What other reasons have you to persuade to this duty?

Answer. Further, let hearers consider how easily without irksomeness they can be present at a play, or at some other profane and idle exercise and discourse of greater length then those sermons which they do so much distaste in respect of the tediousness (as they esteem it) of them, and therefore they ought much more patiently to bear the protracting of time at the performance of such a holy duty.

Question. What else?

Answer. Because this chafing at, and loathing of good things in regard of their length, argues a disordered and ill affected mind. For as loathing and distaste of bodily food is a sign of a sick stomach, so the same loathing, and distasting of spiritual food is a sign of a sinful soul. On the other side, as a hungry appetite, and well relishing of our meat and drink, is a sign of bodily health, so hungering after the wholesome word, and delighting in it, is a sign of a good heart.[53]

Question. What is the last reason?

Answer. The practice, and example of the godly ministers and people in former ages,[54] who have willingly continued a long time together at holy exercises as may appear. How long was the sermon of Christ, the sum and chief points of which are set down in chapters 5-7 of Matthew, and that of Paul in Acts 20:11? Therefore, it is not a strange or new thing for ministers to prolong their speech, and the people their presence with patience and attention.

Question. What is the eleventh duty?

---

[53] Psa. 1:2; Matt. 5:6.
[54] Josh. 8:34-35; Ezra. 8:3.

Answer. That every one bring their own with them, and look to them during the time of the sermon, that they neither walk out of the church, sleep, talk, or commit any unseemly thing.[55]

Question. Is there not some special care of scholars to be had, and such as can write?

Answer. Yes, they are to be accustomed to take sermons in writing.

Question. Why so?

Answer. Because, First, it will cause them to mark, and give ear to the words of the preacher, and keep them both from sleeping, and all unseemly behavior.

Secondly, it will help both their memory and judgement, and enable them to give a better account of what they have heard, both for the good of themselves and others.

---

[55] "Let all things be done decently and in order," (1 Cor. 14:40).

CHAPTER 4:
Duties After the Sermon is Ended

Question. Is not the hearer discharged of his duty when he has heard the whole sermon attentively?

Answer. No, although there is scarcely one of a hundred who does not think so.

Question. What then is to be done?

Answer. First, men are not to go out of the church so soon as the sermon is ended, but stay through the prayer, sacraments, singing of psalms and blessing when they are administered.

Question. Why so?

Answer. Touching on prayer, it is one principal part of the worship of God in the public assemblies, and cannot be despised in this way without sinning. Besides, it is the exercise by which all things are blessed and sanctified to us. Finally, how can we receive so great a blessing at God's hands, and depart from his presence without giving thanks?

Question. What other reason is there?

Answer. If it would be counted a thing uncomely, and undutiful, to stand before an earthly king as a dead image, and soon as his speech was ended, to turn your back on him without any request or thanksgiving. How much more to deal in this way with him that is King of Kings and Lord of Lords?

Question. Why must we stay for the sacraments?

Answer. Because they are the public seals of the mutual covenant between God and us, by which he binds himself to be our God, and we ourselves to be his people. Therefore, we are to be present, not only at the Lord's Supper, which belongs to all believers that are of discretion to examine themselves. But also, at the administration of baptism, by which the same Covenant of Grace and forgiveness of sin is sealed to us.

Question. Is it requisite for me of years to be present at catechizing?

Answer. Yes, for first, many are men in years, which are babes in knowledge.

Secondly, it is a thing of good example, both for the encouragement of youth, and also of the minister himself when he shall see them present that can judge of his pains and labors.

Thirdly, by this means the elder sort shall be better able to examine and confer with the younger at home.

Question. Why must people stay for the blessing?

Answer. Because the Lord, commanding his minister to bless the people, necessarily implies their staying until the blessing is pronounced. Otherwise he should not bless the people, but the bare walls, which would be to take the Name of God in vain.[56]

Question. What is the second duty to be done after the Sermon?

Answer. Such things as have been delivered at church must be, (as it were) chewed by meditation, and turned over again at home after the example of the men of Berea,[57] for quickening our memory, increasing our knowledge, strengthening our faith, *etc.*

Question. What is the third duty?

Answer. Parents and masters must demand, and take account of their people, of the things they have heard.[58]

Question. Why so?

---

[56] "Speak unto Aaron and unto his sons, saying, On this wise ye shall bless the children of Israel, saying unto them, The LORD bless thee, and keep thee: The LORD make his face shine upon thee, and be gracious unto thee: The LORD lift up his countenance upon thee, and give thee peace. And they shall put my name upon the children of Israel; and I will bless them," (Num. 6:23-27).
[57] Acts 17:10-11.
[58] Exod. 12:26; Deut. 6:2, 21; Joshua 4:6.

Answer. Because, first, they are to have a care of their souls as well as of their bodies.

Secondly, they that will win others to godliness, must begin with them sometime, Solomon says.

Thirdly, by this means they shall frame in them more by way of conscience of their duty in civil matters, and in the ordinary works, and labors of their calling.

Question. What is the fourth duty?

Answer. To confer to the godly of that which has been taught, by the way, at our tables; and not according to the wicked custom of a great number, to fall presently into idle and unsavory speeches, or discourses of worldly matters. Yes, to scoffing, and carping at the doctrine, or at its teacher.

Question. What profit will come by this?

Answer. By such godly speeches Christ is after a sort invited and drawn into our company by the presence of his Spirit, as he was to those two Disciples in person that went to Emmaus.[59]

Question. What do you say then to those who do not use this time to speak with one another??

Answer. They are like that part of the natural body, which keeping all the food to itself, and not

---

[59] Luke 24:15, 32; Phil. 4:9; Eph. 4:29-30.

imparting the same to the adjoining members, in a short time, corrupts both himself and them.

Question. What is the final duty in this?

Answer. To keep in mind that the Sabbath is not ended as soon as the sermon is done, and therefore, not to meddle with worldly matters. But spend the rest of the time in prayer, reading, repetition, singing of psalms, *etc.,* according to the scope of the fourth commandment. Therefore, they are greatly deceived who think they have sufficiently sanctified the Sabbath, when they have heard a sermon superficially before noon. And they likewise vainly persuade themselves that the sanctification of the Lord's Day consists chiefly in abstaining from the works and labors of their callings, and yet will pass the same day away in diverse vanities, lascivious dance, drinking, and bodily pleasures.

Question. May no bodily labors be performed on the Lords Day?

Answer. Yes, such as are necessarily required for the health, welfare, and defense of ourselves or our neighbor, and could not well be dispatched the day before, nor deferred until the day following. For in such cases the Son of man is Lord of the Sabbath Day, (Matt. 12:8; Mark 2:27). Therefore, the Maccabees did foolishly in suffering themselves to be slain without resistance because it was the Sabbath Day, which error afterwards they decreed to reform (1 Macc. 2:36).

Question. What is the sixth duty?

Answer. If we have heard anything that seemed dark and doubtful to us, not to be discouraged, but to confer with our godly Pastor that we may know the things that differ.[60]

Question. Why must we do this?

Answer. First, we should use the sermon while we live in this world which apply to earthly things, and we should much more ought to apply it to things that concern eternal life.

Secondly, the "priests lips preserve knowledge,"[61] *etc.*

Thirdly, examples teach the same thing.

Question. What is the seventh duty?

Answer. Every godly hearer must sound and search his own heart, and accordingly sentence and censure himself touching that which he has heard, how

---

[60] "And this I pray, that your love may abound yet more and more in knowledge and in all judgment; That ye may approve things that are excellent; that ye may be sincere and without offence till the day of Christ," (Phil. 1:9-10).

[61] Mal. 2:7; Matt. 13:36; John 16:19; Acts 8:34.

far forth he has been rebellious against the same, or yielded obedience to it.

Question. What will this sifting of the heart bring forth?

Answer. If we find a sweet harmony and consent between God's Word and our wills, it will work in us joy and peace of conscience, with thanksgiving to God, whose mere grace, and free gift it is. Otherwise, it ought to humble us, and work that godly sorrow in us which Paul speaks of (2 Cor. 7:10) and cause us to purge out that old leaven spoken of in 1 Cor. 5:7.

Question. What is the eighth duty?

Answer. It is, that all Christians, especially superiors, endeavor to redress and reform such as belong to their care and charge, by a more special applying of such things as are delivered in sermons. They should do this towards their special sins and transgressions, doubts or fears, by which they shall discharge a brotherly duty, and press the other to think more deeply and fruitfully of the things that are taught.

Question. What follows of all this?

Answer. It appears here, first, how hard and excellent a thing it is not only to preach, but also to hear sermons profitably.

Secondly, it shows how far they are out of the way of discharging their duty, who have superficially spent an hour or two either in preaching or hearing.

Question. What then should faithful ministers do?

Answer. They ought with all care to apply themselves to perform this duty of preaching holily and fruitfully.

First, by diligent study and meditation at home.

Secondly, by a zealous delivering of the same in the church.

Thirdly, by prayer, and watching for the profit of their doctrine both in themselves and others.

Question. What may provoke them to this?

Answer. The promises of God's word set down, "Then I said, I have laboured in vain, I have spent my strength for nought, and in vain: yet surely my judgment is with the LORD, and my work with my God," (Isa. 49:4), and in other places.

Question. What must good people do?

Answer. First, prepare themselves with great piety and religion to hear the Word, and to use all reverence and attention in the hearing.

Secondly, to endeavor with this kind of religion to express and practice it in the whole course of their life.

Question. What should move them to doing this?

Answer. Because, as Christ said, "Blessed are they that hear the Word of God, and keep it," (Luke 11:28). And the Apostle says, "The Word," in this way received, "is able to save their souls," (James 1:21).

FINIS

Other books on Preaching and Hearing by Puritan Publications

The Hearer's Duty and Other Works by Christopher Love (1618-1651)

> This rare set of works by Christopher Love covers hearing the sermon as God intended without distraction while you sit in church listening to the preacher. He also covers buying and selling goods as a Christian steward. It is one of his best works.

The Preacher's Charge and People's Duty by John Brinsley (1600-1665)

> This work should be in the hands of every preacher taking the pulpit in contemporary Christendom. It shows not only the manner of preaching by the herald of God, but also focuses on the hearing of the word by the professing Christian believer.

The Art of Faithful Preaching by William Perkins (1558-1602)

> This work by William Perkins is one of the best books written concisely on the art of preaching. A must read by every minister who stands behind the pulpit, as well as for Christians who want to glean profit from reading Scripture effectively.

5 Marks of a Biblical Church by C. Matthew McMahon

> What are the marks of a biblical church? There are 5 marks that demonstrate the church as the pillar and ground of the truth.

Gospel Worship, or, The Right Manner of Sanctifying the name of God in General, in Hearing the Word, Receiving the Lord's Supper, and Prayer by Jeremiah Burroughs (1599-1646)

> This classic work by Burroughs deals with the Regulative Principle: God alone determines the manner in which sinners approach him. This is a life-transforming and Christ-glorifying biblical work.

Rules for Our Walking with God by Jeremiah Burroughs (1599-1646)

> How are Christians to walk with God like Enoch? Are you walking with God as God requires? What does God require of you in order to know whether you walk with him or not?

The Lord's Voice Cries to the City: A Biblical Guide for Hearing the Word of God Preached by C. Matthew McMahon

> Is the preacher doing what he is supposed to in his preaching in order for you to do what you are commanded to do in your duty to hear the word of God rightly?

Christ Inviting Sinners to Come to Him for Rest by Jeremiah Burroughs (1599-1646)

> Along with Gospel Worship, this is the best work Burroughs ever penned. It is one of the best puritan works you will ever read on coming to Christ.

Pastoral Theology or the Theory of the Evangelical Ministry by Alexander Vinet (1797-1847)

What does the Bible say about the office of a pastor? His home life? His work among the poor? His catechizing? His preaching? His prayer life? And so much more...study with Vinet on this most needful topic in our day.

www.ingramcontent.com/pod-product-compliance
Lightning Source LLC
Chambersburg PA
CBHW031632040426
42452CB00007B/798